FRUIT

Jillian Powell

RSVP

RAINTREE
STECK-VAUGHN
P U B L I S H E R S
The Steck-Vaughn Company

Austin, Texas

Titles in the Series

BREAD   EGGS   FISH   FRUIT
MILK   PASTA   POTATOES
POULTRY   RICE   VEGETABLES

Published by Raintree Steck-Vaughn Publishers, an imprint of Steck-Vaughn Company
Everyone Eats™ is a trademark of Steck-Vaughn Company

Library of Congress Cataloging-in-Publication Data
Powell, Jillian.
Fruit / Jillian Powell.
p.   cm.—(Everyone eats)
Includes bibliographical references and index.
Summary: Discusses the history of fruit, how it is prepared, and its nutritional value, and provides recipes for apple and bacon burgers and Banana and pineapple crumble.
ISBN 0-8172-4765-3
1. Fruit—Juvenile literature.
[1. Fruit.]
I. Title. II. Series: Powell, Jillian. Everyone eats.

Printed in Italy. Bound in the United States.
1 2 3 4 5 6 7 8 9 0 01 00 99 98 97

Picture acknowledgments
Cephas 4, 6 (top), 9 (top), 11 (left), 12, 14 (both), 15 (top), 16 (bottom), 17 (both), 18 (bottom), 19 (both), 20 (both), 21 (both), 22 (both), 23 (both), 24; Chapel Studios 5 (top), 8–9 (bottom), 10 (right), 25 (bottom); Cranberry Information Bureau/Ocean Spray Cranberries Ltd. 7 (bottom) and 15 (bottom); James Davis Travel Photography 10 (left); Dried Fruit Information Service 13 (bottom), 16 (top); Mary Evans 7 (top), 8 (left), 25 (top); Eye Ubiquitous 5 (bottom), 11 (right); Michael Holford 6 (bottom); Wayland Picture Library title page, contents page, 13 (top and middle), 18 (top).

Contents

Fantastic Fruit

Fruit is one of our oldest and most varied natural foods. Fruit comes in every size, shape, and color, from tiny black currants to watermelons bigger than footballs.

A fruit is the fleshy part that protects the seeds of a plant. Some foods that we think of as vegetables are really fruit. They include tomatoes, olives, avocados, and cucumbers. Rhubarb, which we use as a fruit, is really a vegetable, because the stem of the plant is the part that we eat.

Different types of fruit have different tastes and appearances. Some fruits, like apples, are hard and crunchy. Others, like peaches and mangoes, are soft and juicy. Some have smooth skins that we can eat, like grapes, cherries, and plums. Others have to be peeled, like oranges, lemons, bananas, and pineapples.

Fruits grow on trees and bushes. Fruit is an important food for people and for wild animals and birds.

Fruit can be eaten in many different ways. It can be served raw or cooked and in sweet or spicy dishes. Fruit can be used in soups, stews, salads, jellies, and desserts. Or it can be squeezed for juice and fruit drinks.

▲ Nuts are a dry kind of fruit with a hard shell. These are almonds growing on a tree in Sri Lanka.

Although many fruits are good to eat, some kinds of berries and fruits can be poisonous. Never eat a fruit unless you know that it is safe to eat. Some people get sick after eating certain fruits or nuts. We say they are allergic to those foods.

◀ Watermelon contains up to 90 percent water, which makes it refreshing to eat, especially in hot weather.

The First Fruits

People have been eating fruit for thousands of years. The earliest peoples gathered the fruit and nuts of wild plants. By about 4000 B.C., fruits, including dates, figs, grapes, olives, and pomegranates, were being grown and harvested.

The ancient Greeks and Romans used fruit to sweeten fish and meat dishes. Fruit was not usually eaten raw because doctors believed it caused disease. The Romans learned how to dry and preserve fruits. They turned grapes into raisins and wine and stored other fruits in clay pots, with honey, salt water, or vinegar.

▲ The date palm is one of the most ancient trees in the world.

▶ The ancient Egyptians grew grapes and learned to ferment them to make wine. This painting in a tomb shows a husband and wife standing under their grapevines.

In the Middle Ages, cooks used dried fruits like prunes, raisins, and currants in meat and fish stews and pies as well as cakes and puddings. Doctors still believed raw fruit was dangerous. When a very dangerous disease called the plague was spreading in London, the sale of fresh fruit in the street was banned.

In the 16th century, fruit was preserved in sugar and used in jam, jelly, and a dish called flummery, which was made with spiced cream and formed in a mold.

In the 16th century, highly colored fruit dishes were in fashion. Quinces and pears were cooked with red wine, and apple pies were made green by stewing the apples in copper pans with vine leaves. Acid from the fruit reacted with the metal of the pan to turn the fruit green.

People picking grapes at a French vineyard in the 15th century.

Cranberries first grew wild in North America. The Native Americans used them for food and medicine and to dye clothes and feathers. They showed the Pilgrims where to gather cranberries, and they feasted on them at the first Thanksgiving in 1621. Cranberries are still a traditional part of the Thanksgiving meal in the United States.

Fruit in the Past

In the 18th century, doctors realized that raw fruit was a healthful food. By the end of the century, the British navy was giving lemon and lime juice to sailors on long sea voyages, to keep them from getting scurvy, a disease caused by lack of Vitamin C.

◀ In the 18th century, orange sellers like this woman sold oranges as snacks in the street and in theaters.

In cooking, desserts called "fools" were made with fresh fruit, milk, and cream. Quinces, pears, and plums were made into marmalade, which was often so thick that it had to be cut with a knife. Fashionable fruit desserts included melon dyed green with spinach juice and peaches poached in red wine or cochineal (a red dye from a kind of beetle).

These stone pineapples are a symbol of wealth. Along with grapes they are carved on the gates of a vineyard in France.

Pineapples were first brought to Europe from South America in the 16th century. They became very popular in England, and rich people grew pineapples in hothouses.
A pineapple on a coat of arms or a gatepost was a symbol of wealth. In the 1870s, pineapples began to arrive fresh from the West Indies on steamships.

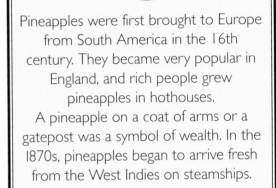

Rich fruitcakes began to be made for celebrations like birthdays, weddings, and Christmas. With the arrival of more tropical fruits on steamships in the 19th century, and the invention of canning by about 1900, the range of available fruits increased.

Pears being poached in red wine to turn them red. This dish was popular in the 18th century.

What Is Fruit?

A fruit is the part of a plant that protects the seeds. Fruit grows when the flowers have been fertilized. Male pollen grains fertilize the ovule (the female part of a flower), producing a seed. A fruit then grows to protect and feed the seed. Nuts protect their seed or kernels inside hard shells.

▲ Wild birds and animals, like this gray squirrel, eat fruit, nuts, and seeds. They spread the seeds around by passing them through their bodies.

Some fruits can grow in most countries of the world. Others need a certain climate to grow well. Tropical fruits like bananas, pineapples, and mangoes need lots of rain and hot sunshine to grow. Fruits like apples, pears, and raspberries grow in much cooler, temperate climates. Dates grow in hot, dry desert lands.

◄ Bananas are grown on plantations in tropical countries. Each tree can bear up to 200 bananas in clusters called "hands."

Fruits can be grouped into families. The citrus family, for example, contains oranges, lemons, limes, and grapefruit. We can also group together hard and crunchy fruits or soft and juicy fruits.

Fruits like plums, peaches, and avocados have one big seed or stone inside. Others, like apples, melons, and grapes, have lots of pips or seeds. Berries are fruits that contain small seeds inside their soft flesh. They include tomatoes, gooseberries, raspberries, and black currants. Their seeds are so tiny that we can eat them.

◀ Apricots come from the group of fruits that contain one hard stone. Inside the stone is a soft kernel.

▶ Some fruits, like these pomegranates, kiwi fruits, and passion fruit have small edible seeds.

The Food in Fruit

Fruit provides a healthful snack or part of a meal and is refreshing and good to eat.

Fresh fruits contain substances called antioxidants (including Vitamins C and E), which help keep our body cells healthy and prevent disease.

Different fruits contain different nutrients but most contain lots of the vitamins and minerals we need to keep us healthy.

Bananas are a good source of energy because they are rich in carbohydrate. They also contain Vitamins A, B, and C.

Fruits like apples, pears, pawpaws, and strawberries contain fiber, which helps us to digest food and pass it through our bodies.

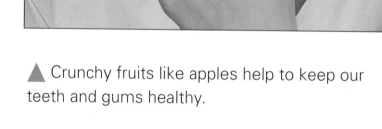

▲ Crunchy fruits like apples help to keep our teeth and gums healthy.

Tennis players often eat bananas during long matches. That is because bananas contain lots of potassium, which helps to avoid cramps.

Apples contain a chemical called pectin, which helps to protect against heart disease caused by too much cholesterol in our bodies. The pectin gets into the bloodstream and sticks to the cholesterol, helping the blood to flow around the body.

12

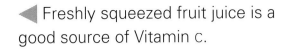 Freshly squeezed fruit juice is a good source of Vitamin C.

▼ Fruits containing lots of Vitamin C include citrus fruits like these, as well as kiwi fruits, red currants, and black currants. Vitamin C helps us fight colds and other illnesses.

Nuts and avocados are rich in protein, which we need to grow and repair our bodies. Vegetarians, who choose not to eat meat, may eat nuts, instead of meat, to give them protein. Nuts contain more fat and are higher in calories than other fruits, which are mostly low in calories.

◀ Fruits that are high in sugar include dates and dried fruits like these raisins. They are a good source of energy.

How Fruit Grows

Fruit is grown all over the world, in gardens, orchards, fruit farms, and plantations. It also grows wild in forests, woods, and fields.

Fruit trees and bushes are planted and pruned in the winter, when they have no leaves. Farmers use animal manure or chemicals to feed fruit plants, which helps them to produce a good crop.

In the spring, when fruit trees and bushes come into flower, farmers must make sure the flowers are fertilized. Some farmers keep bees to carry pollen from flower to flower.

Once fruits have formed, the farmer may spray the plants with chemicals to fight pests and diseases. "Organic" farmers prefer not to use chemicals because they believe the chemicals can harm people and the environment.

▲ A man pruning apple trees in Japan. Pruning allows light and air to reach new shoots, which start to grow in spring.

▶ Peach trees in an Italian orchard being sprayed to prevent pests and diseases.

Sunshine helps fruit to grow and ripen. Some fruits, such as strawberries, ripen in the summer. Others, like apples and pears, ripen in the autumn. It is important to pick fruit at the right time. Fruits like pineapples are picked when they are ripe and sweet. Other fruits, like bananas, are picked when they are unripe, because they continue to ripen after picking. Grapes have to be picked when they contain the right amount of sugar for wine making.

It is very important that fruit trees and bushes have enough water. In dry weather, farmers may have to water their crops.

All fruit must be picked carefully so that it is not damaged. Some fruit can be harvested by special machines that shake the bushes and gather the fruit. Many fruits are picked by hand.

Fruit must be stored in cool, dry sheds. Some farmers spray it with chemicals to preserve it. Fruit may be washed and dried by warm air before being sorted by size, weight, and quality. Packers check the fruit before packing it in boxes to be sold or taken to factories for processing. Fruit must be transported quickly so that it stays fresh.

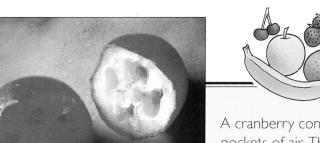

A cranberry contains four pockets of air. This means that it can float. Sometimes, farmers harvest cranberries by flooding the fields. The cranberries are knocked off the plants and a machine skims the floating cranberries off the top of the water.

Preserving Fruit

There are many ways of preserving fruit once it has been picked. If it is not preserved, bacteria will feed on sugar in the fruit and it will rot.

Bacteria need water to live, so one way of preserving fruit is to dry it. Fruit such as dates, figs, apples, and pears can be dried in the sunshine or in hot-air tunnels. This removes up to 75 percent of the water from the fruit. Dried fruit is more chewy than fresh fruit, and is very nutritious. Dried fruit may be ready to eat or may need soaking in water before use.

Lemon juice can be used to stop sliced fruit from turning brown when it reacts with air. The acidity in the citrus juice also improves flavor.

◄ Raisins and currants are different types of dried grapes.

▼ In the hot sun of Victoria, Australia, these grapes are being dried to make raisins.

Fruit can be preserved by sugar. Candied fruit like this has had most of its water replaced by sugar. Making jam or marmalade is another way of preserving fruit by using sugar.

Fruit may be canned in sugar syrup or fruit juice. The fruit is partly cooked then sealed in airtight metal cans, which are heated to kill bacteria.

Some fruits can be frozen. Raspberries and cherries freeze well, but other fruits like strawberries can lose their shape and texture.

Tomatoes being prepared for canning at a factory in Italy.

Fruit can be bottled in vinegar, wine, or spirits or made into spicy chutneys and pickles. Rumtopf is a German pot of fruits preserved in rum. In the West Indies, tropical fruits are bottled with rum and spices, and pickled limes are sold as snacks in the street.

Fruit Products

Fruit is processed into many different products at food-processing factories. The fruit is cooked or dried and used in pies, tarts, cookies, cakes, puddings, mousses, fools, yogurt, and ice cream.

Fruit may also be crushed and used to make jelly, sauces, ketchup, jam, and marmalade. Fruit pulp, which is left over when fruits have been crushed, is used in animal feed. Lemon oil may be used in cosmetics or household cleaners such as dishwashing liquid.

Some fruits, like raspberries, can be used to make vinegar and fruit teas. Fruit juice is packed in bottles or cartons and used to make different kinds of fruit drinks.

▲ Dried fruits are often added to breakfast cereals like this muesli. Some people also like to add slices of fresh fruit to their cereals.

▶ A selection of colorful fruit juice drinks.

A machine crushing apples for cider.

To make cider, yeast is added to apple juice, which is then left to ferment in cider vats for several weeks. Some cider is distilled to make apple brandy, called calvados in France, and applejack in the United States. Wine is made by crushing grapes and adding yeast, which ferments the sugar in the fruit, turning it to alcohol.

Nuts are roasted and crushed for use in ice cream, yogurt, nougat, patés, nutburgers, and sausages. The oil from nuts is used for cooking, and to make margarine, soap, hand cream, paint, and varnish. Almonds and coconut are crushed to make a kind of milk.

Coconut flesh and milk can be used for cooking fish and meat, and in candy, cakes, and cookies. Coconut oil is used in cosmetics such as soap and hand cream, and the thick fiber, called coir, can be used to make mats, rope, and garden compost.

Fruit jams, made by cooking summer fruits with sugar.

19

Cooking with Fruit

There are many simple ways of cooking fruit. Fruits like apples and bananas can be baked in the oven or fried in a little butter.

Pears, apples, and softer fruits like apricots and peaches can be poached in juice, syrup, or wine. Many fruits can be stewed with sugar or honey until they are soft.

Nuts can be roasted in an oven or toasted under the grill. Cashew nuts must be roasted before they are safe to eat.

▲ Apples can be cored and filled with dried fruit, butter, sugar, and spices and baked in the oven for a delicious dessert.

▼ Banana fritters made of bananas fried with butter and sugar.

Fruit is made into many kinds of sweet dishes all over the world, such as American blueberry muffins and apple pie, German Black Forest cake, Austrian strudel, and Danish pastries. Fruit is also used in ice cream, yogurt, mousses, gelatin desserts, fruit salad, sauces, cookies, and candy.

In Eastern, Indian, African, and Caribbean cooking, fruit is used in many savory dishes. Unripe fruits, including pawpaws, mangoes, bananas, and plantains are used in soups, stews, and curries. In the East, fish and meat are often cooked in coconut milk.

In the Middle East, apricots and prunes are cooked with lamb, and soups and stews are flavored with pomegranate juice or whole lemons and limes. Fruits like quinces may be stuffed with spicy meat fillings.

In Western cooking, fruit for savory dishes is used mainly in sauces, such as cranberry sauce with turkey, applesauce with pork, and cherries with duck. Ham may be served with pineapple, and lemon is used to flavor and garnish fish.

▲ Sweet and savory flavors go together well in this dish made with duck and apricots.

Pineapple, pawpaw, and kiwi fruit can all help to make meat more tender because they contain chemicals that can break down protein. These fruits cannot be used fresh in gelatin because the chemicals prevent the gelatin from setting.

◄ West Indian dishes flavored with bananas and limes.

Fruit Dishes from Around the World

In eastern Europe, Germany, and Scandinavia, fruit is made into soups, such as Hungarian cherry soup and German "heaven and earth" soup made with apples and potatoes.

In Africa, soup is made with bananas or pawpaws. Bananas, plantains, and coconuts are used in chicken and beef stews. Plantain chips are more popular than potato chips.

▲ Clafoutis, a French dish made by baking black cherries in a rich pancake batter.

The Caribbean dish of Creole bananas is made of bananas cooked with salt fish, pork, onions, tomatoes, peppers, and coconut milk. Popular desserts include lime pie, pawpaw custard, and guavas cooked in sugar syrup, served with salty cheese.

▶ The Mexican dish of guacamole is made by crushing avocados with tomatoes, chili peppers, lemon juice, and garlic.

In the West Indies, pickled limes are chopped into salads and eaten with fried shark. Pepper mangoes are a popular street snack made by bottling mangoes with chilis in salted water.

In Asia, meals often end with fresh fruit. In Korea, slices of fruit are eaten with small forks from a dish in the middle of the table. In Thailand, chefs carve fruits like pawpaws and mangoes into beautiful flower shapes.

▼ This Moroccan tajgine is made of lamb, cooked in a clay pot with quinces. It may also be made with apples or pears.

▲ A feast of Caribbean dishes, including pineapple and lime salad, lime tart with coconut, and lime gelatin.

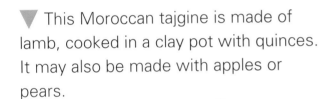

Faisinjan is a Middle Eastern dish of duck or lamb cooked with walnuts and pomegranate juice. Mishmishaya is a traditional recipe for lamb stewed with apricots.

American Waldorf salad is made with apples, walnuts, celery, raisins, and lettuce.

The Russian Easter cake Pashka is made with dried fruits, sour cream, and cream cheese. The cake is baked in a tall mold and decorated with candied fruit.

Legends and Customs

Fruit plays a part in stories, legends, folklore, festivals, and religion. In the Bible, Eve tempted Adam with an apple. Apples appear in classical legends and fairy tales like "Snow White." In Norse and Arab mythology, magic apples have the power to give life forever and even bring people back to life.

In China, peaches are a symbol of living forever and a token of friendship. Mangoes are important in Hindu and Buddhist belief. Buddha meditated in a mango grove.

Pomegranates are an ancient symbol of fertility and wealth in many cultures because of their many seeds. In medieval times, they were pictured on coats of arms and on kings' and priests' robes.

Bobbing for apples is traditional on Halloween, recalling a Roman festival held at the beginning of November to celebrate Pomona, goddess of fruits and seeds. In the United States, pumpkin pie is a traditional dish at the Thanksgiving feast.

▲ These people are dressed up for the Chinese Moon Festival in September, which celebrates an ancient legend. At the festival, moon-shaped fruits like peaches and melons are eaten.

24

Fruit features in many New Year's customs. In the English New Year's tradition of wassailing, people dance and sing around fruit trees, lighting torches and sprinkling the trees with cider or crumbs of food. This is to feed the trees and help them make more fruit.

◀ Wassailing apple trees with hot cider in England during the 19th century.

▼ Dried limes hanging on a balcony in India to bring good luck.

At the New Year in India, lemons and limes are left in baskets on doorsteps to bring luck to friends and neighbors. The Chinese eat cherries, apples, and tomatoes because red is a lucky color. In Greece and Spain, it is traditional to eat a grape on each stroke as the clock chimes midnight, to bring 12 months of good luck. In Jewish tradition people dip sliced apples in honey, to bring a sweet New Year.

Fruit Recipes for You to Try

Apple and Bacon Burgers

To serve two to four people, you will need:

2 tablespoons butter
1 small onion, chopped
3 or 4 cold cooked potatoes, mashed
2 apples, peeled, cored, and chopped
4 slices of bacon, chopped
A pinch of salt and pepper
1 small egg, beaten
4 tablespoons cooking oil

1 Ask an adult to help you to melt the butter over low heat in a frying pan. Fry the onion for about 5–10 minutes until it is soft.

2 Put the onion in a bowl with the mashed potato and mix well.

3 Stir in the chopped apples and bacon, and add a pinch of salt and pepper.

4 Now add the beaten egg until the mixture sticks together.

5 Carefully divide the mixture into balls, then flatten each ball into a patty shape.

6 Ask an adult to help you to heat the oil over low heat in the frying pan. Fry the patties on both sides until they are golden.

Serve with fresh vegetables or a salad.

Banana and Pineapple Crumble

To serve four people, you will need:

4 bananas, peeled and cut into chunks
4 slices of fresh or canned pineapple, cut into chunks
The grated rind of an orange
2 tablespoons light or dark brown sugar
$\frac{2}{3}$ cup of flour, whole wheat if possible
5 tablespoons butter
2 tablespoons granulated sugar
2 tablespoons muesli cereal

1 Put the banana and pineapple chunks into a large bowl. Add the brown sugar and orange rind and mix together well.

2 Grease a pie dish with some butter and spread the fruit mix in the dish.

3 Put the flour and butter into another dish. Cut the butter into little pieces and rub it into the flour with your fingers until it looks like crumbs.

4 Add the granulated sugar and muesli and mix together well.

5 Spoon the crumble mix over the fruit. Bake in the oven at 375° F for 25–30 minutes.

Serve hot with yogurt or cream.

Glossary

acidity The level of acid that anything contains.

airtight Sealed so that air cannot get in or out.

allergy A bad reaction to something, such as food, that is not harmful to most people.

bacteria Tiny living things that have only one cell. Some bacteria cause disease, but others can be useful.

calories Measurements of the energy in food.

carbohydrate Starches or sugars that are an important part of our diet.

cholesterol A substance found in our bodies and in some foods.

classical Of the culture of ancient Greece or Rome.

coat of arms A picture that serves as the special mark of a family.

compost Decayed vegetation used as fertilizer.

cosmetics Products to make people look more attractive.

distilled To purify a liquid by a process of heating then cooling.

environment The landscape and the animals, plants, and people who live there.

ferment To cause a chemical change by means of a culture of yeast or bacteria.

fertility The ability of a plant or animal to produce young.

fertilize To bring female and male cells together to make seed or young.

fertilizer Manure or chemicals used on crops to feed the plants.

fiber A substance in some food that helps us to digest it and pass it through our bodies.

folklore Stories, legends, and myths from a certain area or culture.

grove A small wood.

hothouses Heated buildings for growing plants.

kernel The edible center inside a nutshell or fruit stone.

legend A traditional myth or story.

medieval From the period of the Middle Ages.

meditate To think deeply about something.

Middle Ages The time in history from the sixth to the sixteenth century.

minerals Substances found in some foods. We need minerals to keep us healthy.

mythology The traditional stories of a certain culture or area.

Norse From ancient Scandinavia.

nutrients Any of the substances in food that are needed for health.

nutritious Containing nutrients.

organic Produced without the use of chemicals.

Pilgrims A group of people who sailed from England to America and set up a community at Massachusetts in 1620.

plantations Large estates of land where crops are grown.

pollen Fine grains of powder from the male part of a flower.

preserve To prepare something so that it will keep fresh in storage.

processing Preparing products.

protein Part of food we need to build and repair our bodies.

pruned Cut back.

spirits Strong alcoholic drinks.

temperate A region or climate that is neither very hot nor very cold.

tropical A region or climate that has high temperatures and heavy rainfall.

vats Tanks, usually used for holding liquid.

vineyard A plantation of grape vines, usually for winemaking.

vitamins Certain substances in food that we need to keep us healthy.

wholesalers Traders who buy products in large quantities and sell them to supermarkets and stores.

Books to Read

DeBourgoing, Pascale. *Fruit*. First Discovery Books. New York: Scholastic, 1991.

Harris, Colin. *A Taste of West Africa*. Food Around the World. New York: Thomson Learning, 1995.

McKenley, Yvonne. *A Taste of the Caribbean*. Food Around the World. New York: Thomson Learning, 1995.

Moss, Miriam. *Fruit*. Threads. Ada, OK: Garrett Educational Corporation, 1995.

Nottridge, Rhoda. *Apples*. Food We Eat. Minneapolis, MN: Lerner Group, 1991.

Wake, Susan. *Citrus Fruits*. Food We Eat. Minneapolis, MN: Lerner Group, 1990.

Index

Numbers in **bold** show subjects that appear in pictures.